THAT'S WHAT'S DIFFERENT ABOUT ME!

That's What's Different About Me!

Story and Coloring Book

Illustrated by Kathryn Robbins

APC

Autism Asperger Publishing Co.
P.O. Box 23173
Shawnee Mission, Kansas 66283-0173
www.asperger.net

© 2006 Autism Asperger Publishing Co.
P.O. Box 23173
Shawnee Mission, Kansas 66283-0173
www.asperger.net

All rights reserved. No part of the material protected by this copyright notice may be reproduced or used in any form or by any means, electronic or mechanical, including photocopying, recording, or by any information storage and retrieval system, without the prior written permission of the copyright owner.

ISBN: 1-931282-97-8

This book is designed in Helvetica Neue, Highlander and Hot Coffee.

Printed in the United States of America.

Preface

As a parent of a child with autism and a primary school teacher, I know how important it is for children with autism spectrum disorders to be better understood by their peers. When children don't know why a child doesn't communicate the same way they do, they are not sure how to play and interact with that child and tend not to include the child in their play. If, on the other hand, children have an understanding of why a child acts or communicates differently, they can learn to be more accepting of those differences and can learn how to communicate and play together.

The Friend 2 Friend Social Learning Society has developed a puppet presentation, *That's What's Different About Me!*, that help children (and adults) understand their peers who have autism spectrum disorders. As a presenter for Friend 2 Friend I have seen first-hand how the kids enjoy the puppet play and, more important, how effective the presentations are in starting the journey towards understanding, empathy and friendships.

This book is an exciting accompaniment to the *That's What's Different About Me!* program. By telling the puppets' story, this beautifully illustrated book reinforces the message presented in the play. As children read, color and reread the book, they will gain a better understanding of their peers with differences and will become more comfortable including friends with autism in their play.

— Janet Cregan, BGS-PDP
Friend 2 Friend Program Guide/Parent

"Hi, my name is Crystal. This is my friend Angela, and this is my other friend, Freddie. You know, last year Freddie and I didn't play together very much, but now we do. Would you like to hear the story of how Freddie and I became better friends? It all started one day when Angela and I where playing *Trouble* ..."

"Your move, Crystal," Angela said as she pointed to the *Trouble* game. I was just about to take my turn when our teacher, Mrs. Beaks, called. "Angela, it's time to finish your math."
"Okay, Mrs. Beaks," Angela said as she stood up to leave. "I've got to go, Crystal. I'll come back when I'm done with my math, okay?"
"Okay," I answered.

I was feeling kind of bored, so I looked around the classroom for someone else to play with. I saw Freddie sitting in the corner drawing. I called to him. "Hey, do you want to play *Trouble* with me? Well, do you, do you?"
"No!" Freddie said as he turned his back on me and put his hand up to hide his face.
I thought Freddie was rude, so I called to my teacher for help. "Mrs. Beaks!"

"Yes, Crystal," answered Mrs. Beaks as she waggled over to me.
"I don't have anyone to play with," I said.
"Did you ask Freddie to play?" asked Mrs. Beaks.
"I tried but uh … well. Freddie is not like the other kids. Why is he different, why is he that way?"
"Everybody is different in his or her own way! Look at me. I have a special wing, so whenever I try to fly, I end up on my beak," said Mrs. Beaks as she proudly flapped her wings but dropped to the floor. **"That's what's different about me."**

Once Mrs. Beaks had picked herself off the floor, I asked, "But what's different about me?"
"Well, let's just think about this. What are you good at?" asked Mrs. Beaks.
"I'm good at dancing!" I answered proudly while I danced around the classroom.
"You are a wonderful dancer! Do you think there might be something that you're not so good at?" Mrs. Beaks asked.
"Oh, I know. I'm not very good at math," I sighed as I plunked myself down at my desk.
"That's okay, because we all have things that we're good at – and things that we're not so good at – because **we all have different kinds of minds**," Mrs. Beaks patiently explained.

"How is Freddie's mind different?" I wondered.
Hearing our conversation, Freddie chirped in. "I have the kind of mind that has **autism**."
I had never heard that word before, so I asked Freddie, "What is autism?"
"**Autism makes you think differently than other kids!**" Freddie answered proudly.
"That's true, Freddie," added Mrs. Beaks. "Sometimes you communicate differently than Crystal, which can make it difficult for you to play and make friends. But I bet you really want friends!"
"Yes, I do," Freddie replied, as a smile crept across his face.

I thought I could help Freddie make friends, so I asked Mrs. Beaks, "What can I do to play with Freddie?"
Mrs. Beaks said I could learn to play and make friends with Freddie by using her special tips. "These tips could help you play with Freddie. I call them *friendship tips*," she said.
"What are those friendship tips?" I asked.
"Friendship Tip #1: **Move closer to Freddie and say his name to get his attention** before you start talking," Mrs. Beaks explained as she waddled over to Freddie and put her wing around him.
"Okay, I'll try that. What else?" I asked.

"Friendship Tip #2: **_Use small sentences and speak slowly and clearly_**," Mrs. Beaks explained.

"But why do I need to use small sentences?" I asked.

"Freddie understands words differently than you do. Sometimes too many words can sound like **blah, blah, blah** to him," Mrs. Beaks explained.

"Oh yeah; sometimes too many French words sound like blah, blah, blah to me," I added.

I asked Mrs. Beaks if there was anything else I needed to know to help Freddie. She nodded and started.
"**Use gestures** – like pointing – to help Freddie understand what you are saying. And **wait** – give Freddie time to think about what you are saying and time to answer you."
"I can do all those things. It's a snap!" I said as I snapped my fingers.
"Good job, Crystal. Why don't you give it a try right now!" Mrs. Beaks said encouragingly as she waddled back to her desk.
"Okay," I said and headed over to where Freddie was sitting. "Thanks for the friendship tips, Mrs. Beaks!"
"You're welcome," Mrs. Beaks called over her wing.

I walked over to Freddie, said his name, and used small sentences while pointing to the *Trouble* game. I spoke very clearly. "Would you like to play *Trouble* with me?"
"Yup!" Freddie replied right away.
"Great!" I said as I sat down next to him. "You can be red and I will be yellow; you can go first and I'll go second. Remember: They go this way and ..."
All of the sudden I was rudely interrupted by Freddie announcing, "I'm the host."
"No, there isn't a host in this game. We are both players and ...," I stated.
"No – I'm the host! I'm the host! Ahhhhhhhhhh!" Freddie screamed at the top of his lungs.

"What was that?" I said, jumping back.
Just then, Mr. Monkeybones, a special education assistant, came over. "Hey dude and dudette, what's up?" he greeted us.
"I tried Mrs. Beaks's friendship tips and they didn't work. Freddie just screamed AAAAH!" I told Mr. Monkeybones, a bit annoyed.
"I think Freddie was just feeling frustrated," Mr. Monkeybones reminded me. "Remember Friendship Tip #2: Use small sentences, speak slowly and clearly"?
"Oh yeah, I think I said too many words … blah, blah, blah, blah!" I realized.

"Maybe," Mr. Monkeybones replied, nodding his head. "I have some more friendship tips that might help. Would you like to hear them?"
"Sure."
"Friendship Tip #3: **Watch Freddie to learn the things that he likes to do,**" explained Mr. Monkeybones.
I realized that I already knew some of the things Freddie liked to do, so I said, "I know what Freddie likes to do – drawing, computers, videos, DVDs …!"

"That's great," Mr. Monkeybones responded encouragingly. "Then you are all set for Friendship Tip #4, which is "**Give Freddie choices of the things he likes to do!**"
"Hey, I know another friendship tip!" I said excitedly.
"What's that?" asked Mr. Monkeybones.

"Friendship Tip #5: *I can ask Freddie questions like* … Will you sit beside me? or Will you play with me?" I explained. "Wow, cool idea, Crystal!" Mr. Monkeybones said encouragingly. "And here is one more. Friendship Tip #6: *Use friendly*

words like 'good job' and 'give me five,'" continued Mr. Monkeybones.
"Give me five, Monkeybones!" I said as I raised my hand up in the air.
"Cool, Crystal, here's a hairy five," Mr. Monkeybones said as he raised his paw to greet my high five. "Well, it's time for my cappuccino break. See ya later, dudes!" Mr. Monkeybones said as he meandered out of the classroom with a wave.

Rehearsing all the friendship tips in my head, I decided to give it another try. So I went over to Freddie and said, "Freddie, what are you doing?" Freddie did not answer. Instead, he made a very strange sound while tapping his head.
"Squawk, Squawk, Squawky, Squawk" came the sound from Freddie.
"What was that sound?" I asked.
"That is my self-regulating behavior," answered Freddie.
"Your what?" I asked, noticing that Angela had come back from finishing her math.
"Oh, that's just Freddie's stim," Angela confirmed.

"You know, **self-regulating behaviors or 'stims'** – Mrs. Beaks told us all about them," Angela explained. "Everybody has stims. Look, you are doing one now!"
"Oh?" I said, taking my fingers out of my mouth. "I suck my fingers; that must be my stim."
"Yeah, and I twirl my hair," Angela stated, lowering her voice to a whisper as she added, "and I sometimes I even pick my nose. And Freddie makes a squawking sound – that's his stim."
"Why do we do stims anyway?" I asked.
"We do stims when we're concentrating, when we're trying to calm down and sometimes when we're trying to stay awake – like in math," Angela answered with a laugh.

"You know, Angela, Freddie is different than me in a lot of ways. But that's okay, because everybody is different in his or her own way," I stated with confidence.

Angela nodded her head in agreement, adding, "Yeah and *being a good friend means accepting differences.*"

"You're right, so I'm going to try again," I said as I walked over to Freddie.

"Freddie?" I began, as I pointed to the *Trouble* game and then at Freddie's computer. "Would you like to draw or play *Trouble*?" Freddie looked at me. Then he looked at the *Trouble* game and then at his computer. He seemed to be thinking about the options. Then he answered, "Draw."
"Can I draw with you?" I asked as I pointed to the computer.
"Sure," Freddie replied.
Angela came over. "Freddie, what are you drawing?" she asked
"Sponge Bob," Freddie replied.
"Freddie, can I see your Sponge Bob drawing?" I asked joining in.

"Sure," Freddie said as he turned his computer around so Angela and I could see his masterpiece.
"Wow, that is the best Sponge Bob drawing I have ever seen!" I exclaimed, marveling at Freddie's drawing. "Freddie, will you show Angela and me how to draw Sponge Bob?"
"Okay!" answered Freddie.
Angela, Freddie and I spent the rest of the morning drawing and playing together.
And that's the story of how Angela, Freddie and Crystal all became good friends.

Seven Basic Friendship Tips

The Friend 2 Friend program introduces children to prosocial communication techniques to help them interact successfully with their peers with autism. These techniques, called *Seven Basic Friendship Tips,* include communication tools that children may use with all their peers; they have been found to be especially effective when interacting with a child with autism.

1. **Get Your Friend's Attention** – Move closer and say your friend's name before you start to speak.

2. **Use Small Sentences, Gestures, and Wait** – Use small sentences and gestures – like pointing – to help your friend understand you. Then wait to give your friend time to answer you.

3. **Watch Your Friend** – Watch your friend to learn the things that he or she likes to do or is good at.

4. **Give Your Friend Choices** – When asking your friend to play, give your friend choices of the things you know he or she likes to do.

5. **Ask Your Friend to Talk** – Ask your friend questions like, "Will you sit beside me?" "Will you play with me?"

6. **Use Friendly Words** – When speaking to your friend, use friendly words like "Good job" or "Give me five."

7. **Accept Differences** – Everybody is different in his or her own way. Being a good friend means accepting differences.

Seven Basic Friendship Tips

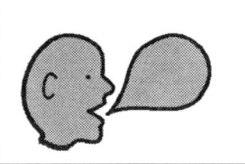
1. Get Your Friend's Attention

2. Use Small Sentences, Gestures; Wait

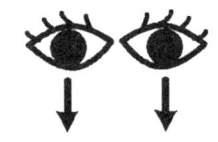
3. Watch Your Friend

4. Give Your Friend Choices

5. Ask Your Friend to Talk

6. Use Friendly Words

7. Accept Differences

The Picture Communication Symbols, used with permission from Mayer-Johnson Inc., PO Box 1579, Solana Beach, CA 92075, 800 588 4548 (phone) URL www.mayer-johnson.com

Pick one of the friendship tips and draw and color a story to go with it.

To order additional copies:

THAT'S WHAT'S DIFFERENT ABOUT ME! – STORY AND COLORING BOOK

Single copies: $4.95

Classroom sets; 10 or more: $3.50 each

NAME _____

ADDRESS _____

CITY _____

STATE _____ ZIP _____

PHONE _____ EMAIL _____

APC Autism Asperger Publishing Company

To order, call **913-897-1004**, fax to **913-681-9473**,
visit our website at **www.asperger.net**
or mail to **AAPC** • P.O. Box 23173
Shawnee Mission, KS 66283-0173

CODE	TITLE	PRICE	QTY	TOTAL
9969	That's What's Different About Me Story and Coloring Book; single copies	$4.95		
9969	That's What's Different About Me Story and Coloring Book; classroom sets; 10 or more	$3.50 each		

SHIPPING AND HANDLING

Order Total	Ground
$1 – $50	$5
$51 – $100	$8
$101 – $200	$10
$201 – $300	$20
$301 – $400	$30
Over $400	$40 + 1% of subtotal

METHOD OF PAYMENT
❑ AMEX ❑ VISA ❑ DISCOVER ❑ MASTERCARD ❑ P.O. ATTACHED
❑ CHECK/MONEY ORDER ENCLOSED (PAYABLE TO AAPC)

ACCOUNT # ☐☐☐☐☐☐☐☐☐☐☐☐☐☐☐☐

EXP. DATE ☐☐ — ☐☐ SIGNATURE _____

SUBTOTAL $ _____

7.5% KS SALES TAX + _____
(Kansas Residents Only)

SHIPPING & HANDLING + _____

TOTAL _____

(Required to process your order)

APC

Autism Asperger Publishing Co.
P.O. Box 23173
Shawnee Mission, Kansas 66283-0173
www.asperger.net